Doune Castle

Doreen Grove
Principal Inspector of Ancient Monuments

The builder of Doune Castle had royal pretensions. Robert Stewart, Duke of Albany and governor of Scotland on behalf of his feeble brother, Robert III, was ever hopeful of becoming king himself one day. Doune remains a lasting testimony to the man known to history as 'Scotland's uncrowned king'.

Only with Albany's death in 1420 did Doune finally gain the status its builder had desired - it became a kingly residence. And so it remained for the next 200 years, a royal retreat from the burdens of state.

Seal of Robert Stewart, Duke of Albany, Earl of Fife and Menteith.

Doune Castle from the north west (David Simon).

A Guided Tour

'The Banner'd Towers o' Doune'

This tour guides the visitor around the castle, beginning with a walk around the outside of the forbidding castle walls and ending at the very top of the 'banner'd towers o' Doune'. You may, however, prefer to start your tour at the gatehouse entrance (page 8) and leave your walk around the defences until later.

Doune Castle was designed with two purposes in mind - to provide a residence fit for a king's brother, a visible statement of its owner's wealth and standing in society. It also had to be strong enough to enable the owner to defend his vast and wealthy estate, the earldom of Menteith.

Exceptionally at Doune we have a castle that was planned in a single episode. Almost all other great castles surviving to this day are the work of many hands over several centuries. Although there are indications that the builder, Robert Stewart, Duke of Albany, changed his mind during construction, and that his grand scheme remained incomplete at his death in 1420, Doune Castle is essentially one coherent design. This gives us a wonderful opportunity to see what the leading man of his day in Scotland felt was appropriate for his needs and aspirations in an age when the conspicuous display of wealth and status was seen as vital in maintaining authority and good governance.

River Teith

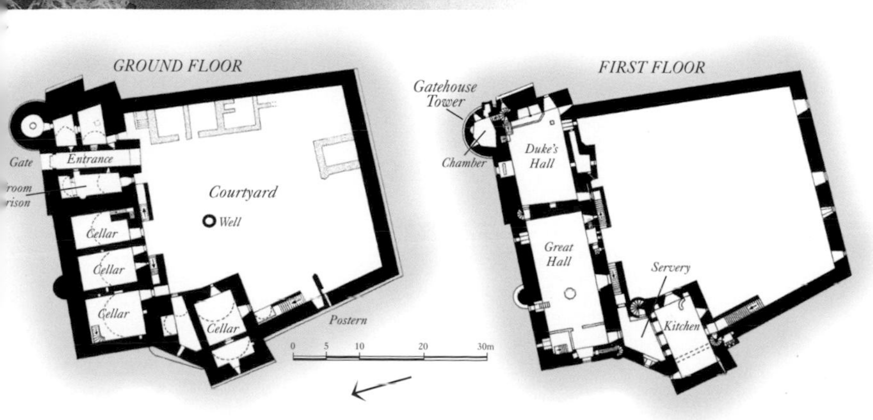

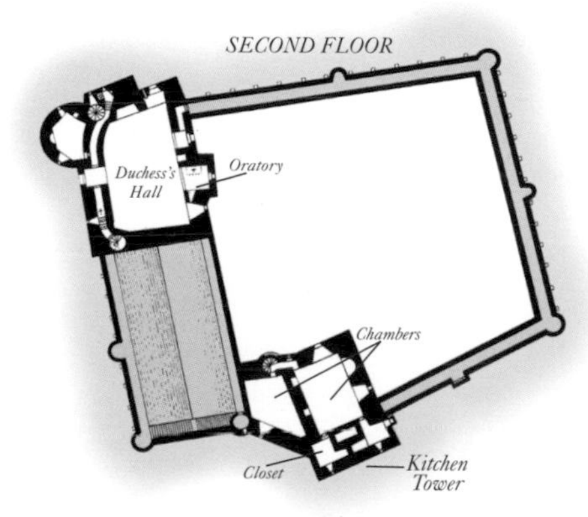

Plans of the castle over the three main floors of accommodation.

A walk around the walls

To appreciate the setting and scale of Doune Castle, it is worth walking around the walls before entering.

The castle sits atop a mound at the neck of a promontory, wedged between the Ardoch Burn (on the left) and the River Teith (on the right). Behind the castle (that is, to the south) are banks and ditches that may have been intended to impede an army approaching from that side. They may though be landscape features; without excavation we just cannot say.

The Gatehouse Tower

As you approach the entrance, the mighty **gatehouse tower** soars above you fully 30 m (100 ft.) in height. Like the rest of the castle, its coursed rubble walls are built of the local dark-coloured sandstone whilst the lighter coloured sandstone used for the finer architectural details, such as the window openings, was quarried at Ballengeich, in the shadow of Stirling Castle, 5 miles (8 km) away.

Above the well-defended entry, and instantly noticeable by the fine windows, were the main apartments of the Duke and Duchess of Albany, spread over three floors. To the left of the entry, at the north-east corner, you will see a smaller **round tower** projecting from the north-east corner of the great tower. This too contained high-quality accommodation, to augment the provision in the main tower. The small window slits light a series of private chambers, one on each floor, most of them *en suite*, that is with a latrine closet attached. As you walk left around this round tower, you will see the latrine closet serving the second-floor room projecting from the wall. The **chute** itself could have discharged more than waste matter, for it may also have been used by defenders to fire down on their attackers.

The tall **rectangular tower** projecting beyond the round tower also contributed to the comfort of the noble residents in the great tower, for it housed the chimney flues heating the main rooms, the main stair that corkscrewed up through the full height of the castle linking those rooms, as well as additional latrine closets. At the very top, on the wall-head where the flagpole now stands, there was probably a beacon basket, used in emergencies to warn those within sight of impending danger.

Left: The mighty gatehouse tower at the north-west corner (equivalent in height to a 10-storey tower block) dominates the curtain walls of Doune.

Right: The ruin of Albany's latrine closet projects from the gatehouse tower.

A WALK AROUND THE WALLS *continued*

The castle from the south west.

The Curtain Walls

The **east curtain wall** is one mass of masonry, relieved only by the water spouts, parapet and two round turrets that all project from the wall-head. These features most likely date from the large-scale repairs carried out in the 1580s on the orders of the young King James VI.

The **south curtain wall** by contrast is pierced by four fine window openings. You will see, however, when you enter the courtyard that there are no fine rooms behind the wall to benefit from the light they let in. This is one of the many mysteries of Doune - just what had Albany in mind for the south range that he didn't quite get around to building?

The **west curtain wall** is almost featureless too, apart from a small **postern**, a kind of tradesmen's entrance, midway along it. Because this door was a potential weak spot, it is protected from above by a stone box, called a machicolation, projecting from the wall-head. As with the projecting latrine closet further along to the left, the machicolation enabled defenders to fire down on their attackers.

Above: The postern, machicolation and latrine chutes along the west curtain wall.

Right: Water spouts, turret and parapet project from the south-east corner.

Projecting from the west curtain wall is the **kitchen tower**. You will see that the lower part of the tower is constructed slightly differently from the remainder of the castle walls - the body of the wall is built of less regular rubblework than the rest of the castle masonry, and the corners are not built of the usual lighter-coloured stone. This suggests that this part of the castle predates Albany's work of the late fourteenth century. As you skirt carefully around the kitchen tower, notice also the rather awkward connection between the kitchen tower and the buildings to its north, another indication perhaps that the kitchen tower is earlier than the rest.

The **north curtain wall**, unlike the others, has great buildings rising up behind it, the great hall and the gatehouse tower beyond (see the photograph on page 9). This north wall holds clues that Albany changed his mind during the building works. For one thing, the round-headed windows are at varying heights and no two are alike. For another, the solid rounded turret projecting half-way along the wall seems to serve no purpose. The only explanation for its existence is that it was intended to mark the termination of a major cross-wall behind that was never built. If it had been, the great hall would have been divided into two rooms.

The Gatehouse entrance

The entrance passage.

Returning to the gatehouse, you soon realise that Albany was taking no chances with the defence of the main entry into his castle. The outer wooden door is not the original, but the iron **yett** immediately behind it is. Such strong cross-barred gates (*yett* is Scots for a gate) were common features in Scottish castles, the idea being that if the outer wooden door was smashed or burned down, the robust yett behind would hold firm and enable the defenders to fire through the square openings. (Note the complex way that the horizontal and vertical bars intersect, thus adding strength to the structure.) Immediately beyond the yett you will see a long narrow slit in the roof. This feature enabled defenders in the room above to fire down on their attackers breaching the outer door and yett.

There was originally another door midway along the **entrance passage**, and yet another yett at the inner, courtyard end. This yett could be closed from the courtyard side, thereby forestalling the attackers' progress. There was no access from the passage to the upper floors of the gatehouse tower, and the passage's solid stone vault protected the defenders from fire. The only area originally accessible from the passage was the **guard room**, or porter's lodge, on the right-hand (west) side, with a fireplace, a narrow slit for observing the passage, and a small **prison cell**. (The guardroom and cell now serve as the castle shop.) The three stone-vaulted rooms now reached through a door in the east wall of the passage were **storage cellars**, formerly accessible only from the courtyard to the south; two of the cellars have hatches in their ceilings to facilitate moving stores between floors.

Below: The castle from the north west

The Courtyard

Inside the courtyard, you begin to appreciate the extent of Albany's vision. Your attention is immediately drawn to the impressive buildings ranged along the north and west curtain walls - the lofty gatehouse tower through which you entered, with its three floors of noble accommodation; the squatter but equally imposing great hall to its left; and, finally, the kitchen tower in the north-west corner. The upper floors of each of the three buildings were reached by three flights of **stairs** - that into the gatehouse tower hidden from view behind a stone enclosing wall, the other two clearly visible on either side of the kitchen tower.

But what also strikes you is the fact that Albany's vision was never completed. Look at the kitchen tower, for example. The stone 'tusks' projecting from the corner jutting into the courtyard clearly show that another two-storey building was planned for the west side, but apparently never constructed. Similarly, the south curtain wall has large round-headed windows, but alas no buildings to go with them. What was Albany planning for the south range that required such fine windows? A chapel perhaps? Or another suite of noble accommodation? Without excavation it is impossible to say whether the building(s) planned for this area were completed and subsequently demolished (highly unlikely) or were constructed of timber (also unlikely). It is also unclear whether Albany intended to build along the east side of the courtyard also; there are no window openings, and the slight remains of roof raggles, or lines, in the east curtain wall, and the low walls visible probably relate to later buildings.

Below: the four-light window in the courtyard wall of the great hall once bathed the dais, or raised platform, therein in sunlight.

One scenario is that Albany's ultimate vision was for a castle very differently arranged than the one we now admire. The main accommodation, for himself and his duchess, would occupy the whole of the south range, where the rooms and chambers would benefit from the sunnier aspect and the better view overlooking the river. However, given the precarious political situation, Albany chose to make his priority the securing of the castle complex by having the gatehouse tower built first. Once completed, this would at least offer respectable and suitably furnished rooms and chambers for his personal use whilst building work continued on the remainder of the grand scheme, progressing around the courtyard in an anti-clockwise direction, starting with the great hall, the main public reception room in the castle, and continuing with the adjacent kitchen tower, with its mix of service and residential accommodation. Only when the main accommodation in the south range was completed would Albany vacate the gatehouse tower for his new lodging. Thereafter, the gatehouse tower would be given over to Albany's chiefs of staff, including his constable, or keeper, responsible for security, his steward, responsible for managing the extensive household, his marshall who controlled transport arrangements, and his chaplain who looked after secretarial matters as well as the household's spiritual needs. Regrettably, soon after the completion of the kitchen tower, Albany either abandoned his dream, or his dream died with him. That was in 1420 in another great royal castle, Stirling.

Let us now return to what does exist, rather than what might have been. The principal accommodation in all three buildings was on the first floor - the 'piano nobile', or noble floor. The ground floors throughout comprised stone-vaulted **cellars**, or storerooms, each one entered from the courtyard and most connected with the floor above either by a stair or through a hatch. When you consider that most of the rents due from the vast earldom of Menteith were paid not in coin but in meat, grain and timber, it is not hard to imagine the now-empty cellars full to overflowing.

The **well** in the courtyard was largely reconstructed in 1884. The timber windlass, however, includes some of the pieces found in the well-shaft, which is some 20 m deep.

The Kitchen Tower

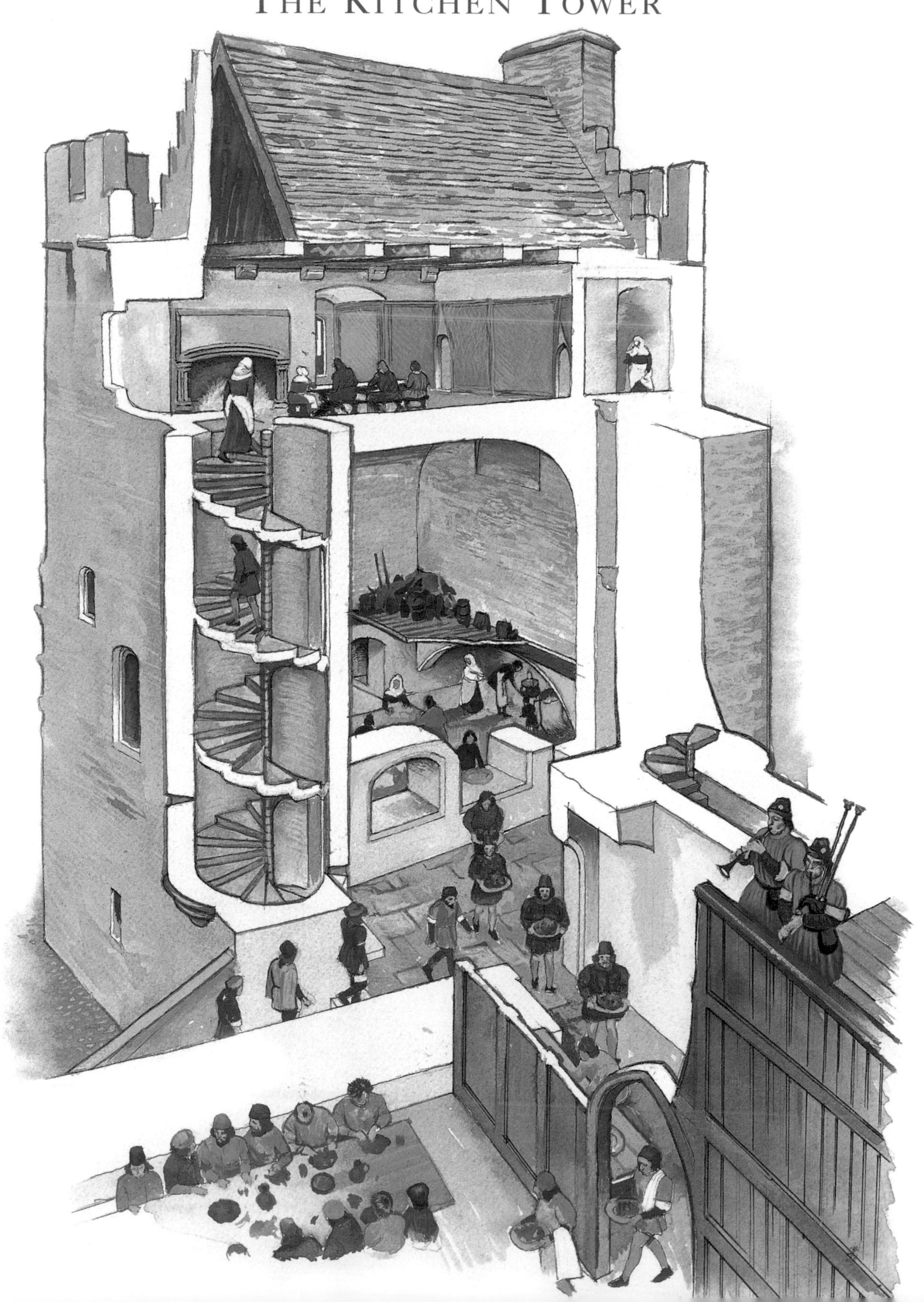

Climb the **stair** in the north-west corner of the courtyard, where the great hall and kitchen tower meet. This stair would have been used by guests attending feasts in the great hall, or tenants of the earldom dancing attendance on their lord. Inside, you enter an irregular space that was the **servery**. Note the two serving hatches on the left, through which the fattest roast hog or the grandest stuffed swan was passed on its way from the kitchen to the great hall.

Above: The two serving hatches and kitchen beyond, pictured from the doorway leading from the great hall.

The **kitchen** itself was on the first floor of the kitchen tower. A large, low-arched fireplace fills one side of the room, a window brings light in from the north and, on the left-hand side, are two slop-drains. Kitchen fireplaces in medieval times were working spaces as well as cooking stances, not least for the turnbrochie, the lad whose job it was to rotate the great roasting spit. The kitchen has a high stone barrel-vault with smoke-holes above the windows and in the crown of the vault to extract the smoke, fumes and heat. The low footings of a **bread oven** near the big east window are all that remain of the oven built during the 1745 Jacobite Rising. The paving dates from the restoration of 1883. The door in the south wall was clearly intended to connect the kitchen with the planned west range, but would also have been used by the kitchen servants as their access into the kitchen from the courtyard below.

Left: a cut-open reconstruction drawing of the kitchen tower, servery and west (bottom) end of the great hall as they might have been used in Albany's day (David Simon).

Returning to the servery, you will see above you the projecting stone corbels that supported the upper floors. These upper rooms, and those in the upper part of the kitchen tower, are reached from a spiral stair that appears to be an insertion, though it probably replaces an earlier timber stair. If you climb that stair, you will enter one of the best rooms in the castle, directly over the kitchen. The **chamber** has long been known as Mary Queen of Scots' bedchamber, but almost uniquely among the Stewart monarchs, Mary seems never to have visited Doune! The chamber, though, was clearly intended for noble use, perhaps for guests of Albany. Two large windows facing east and south light it, and it has a fine arched fireplace decorated in a similar style to those in the gatehouse tower. Leading from it are two smaller closets, one a sleeping closet and the other a latrine closet; both would have been very cosy situated as they are to either side of the kitchen fireplace flue.

The top floor by contrast is simply a garret, only accessible from the wall-walk. A contemporary plan in the British Museum shows that it was from there that John Home and his fellow prisoners made their escape in 1746.

Below: The chamber (Mary Queen of Scots' Bedchamber) on the upper floor of the kitchen tower. The doorway on the right leads into what was once a sleeping closet.

The Great Hall

The great hall was the main reception and banqueting room in the castle. It was far and away the largest room in the castle, with sufficient volume to fit two or three modern houses inside it!

Entering from the servery end, you come first into the **screens passage**. This is now marked on the floor by a low kerb, but would originally have been a narrow space partitioned off from the great hall by a timber screen. That screen had two functions - it hid the kitchen activity from the 'great and grand' assembled in the hall, and it reduced draughts. A door to the left gave access to a stair leading up to the **minstrels' gallery** (the restored gallery is not as wide as the original) and to the wall-walks. At the far end of the passage was the **buttery**, where the wine and ale brought up from the cellar beneath were dispensed (the word 'buttery' comes from the old French *bouteillerie*, 'bottle store'); the large hatch in the floor opens into the drink cellar.

The great hall as you see it today owes much to the restoration carried out in 1883. That work included the roof high above you, the window glazing, and the furniture at one end. But much remains from Albany's time. Apparently there was evidence for the **firebasket** in the centre of the hall, and the louvred smoke-hole directly above it would have been similar to the medieval arrangement. Five windows, in the west, north and south walls, light the hall, and no two are alike. The finest is the four-light **dais window** at the east end of the south wall, which bathed in sunlight the dais, or raised platform, where the host and his guests sat at the high table. Within the dais window opening is a small **latrine closet**, doubtless for the exclusive use of those same 'high table' guests. And if you look closely at the side walls, above eye level, you will see traces of the hooks from which were suspended the hangings that did so much to bring colour and warmth to the vast hall.

Above: The window at the west end of the great hall formerly lit the screens passage at the west (bottom) end of the great hall, whilst the doorway on its left led to a stair leading down to the cellar below and up to the minstrels' gallery and the castle battlements.

Left: The four-light dais window at the east (top) end of the great hall.

The Gatehouse Tower

A door in the north-east corner of the great hall leads to the chambers in the gatehouse tower. In days gone by, that same door would have been used by the Duke and Duchess of Albany to pass to and from their private apartments in the gatehouse tower. The Albanys could also reach their apartments directly from the courtyard by the enclosed stair to the west of the entrance passage.

Before you explore the gatehouse tower, here is a 'health warning'. In the absence of contemporary documents, such as an inventory of fixtures and furnishings, we have no way of knowing precisely how the Albanys, or subsequent royal residents, used the spaces in the tower. We can only make inspired guesses based on analogies with other lordly residences.

The problem is - the gatehouse tower is of such unusual design that finding appropriate comparisons is exceedingly difficult. One distinct possibility is that each of the two main floors comprised one apartment, one for the Duke on the first floor, and the other for the Duchess on the second floor.

The unusual 'double' fireplace in the Duke's Hall.

The Duke's Hall

The room adjacent to the great hall is known as the **Duke's Hall**. In its heyday it most probably served as a private withdrawing room off the great hall for the exclusive use of Albany and his principal guests. Here they would retire after feasting to partake in private entertainment or discuss important business. The chamber would also have been used for private dinner parties and for holding audiences granted to important visitors.

The present furniture and interior decoration, dating from the 1883 restoration, convey a misleading impression of its original appearance, for the focal point in Albany's day would have been either a great chair of estate and four-poster bed of estate, lavishly draped with coloured hangings; both would have emphasised the exalted status of its owner. The one surviving glory of the chamber is the fireplace. Its double arrangement is not precisely echoed anywhere else; maybe it was designed so that Albany could choose one bar or two!

Other features of historic interest include the stair at the north end of the restored screens passage giving access to the minstrels' gallery and the upper floors and wall-walk. In the sill of the north-facing window you will see a timber flap. Lift it and peer down and you will see what the defending garrison would have seen. (But please don't drop any missiles; we welcome our visitors today.) In the south wall a door in the right-hand window leads into a small **closet**, with a stone basin draining to the outside.

Left: This reconstruction drawing shows how the Duke's Hall may have looked around 1400 (David Simon).
The Duke of Albany (the only person seated) grants an audience to another person of high rank. The Duke's great bed and chair of estate, the brightly-coloured hangings and the display of fine plate would all have accompanied Albany wherever he went, leaving this hall bare in his absence.

Steps in the north wall lead down to an odd shaped chamber, the first of several formed within the projecting round tower. This chamber is differently arranged from the others above; it has no fireplace but it does have a hatch in the floor linking it with the cellar beneath. This suggests that it was not a sleeping closet, but a service room for the Duke's Hall.

Below: The Duke's Hall as it appears today, following the 1883 'restoration'.

The Gatehouse Tower

continued

The gatehouse tower from the battlements atop the east curtain wall.

The Duke's and Duchess's Chambers

A flight of steps in the north-west corner of the Duke's Hall leads to the upper floors. The first chamber you come to is the next room up in the round tower. This chamber does have a good fireplace, a fine lancet window, and a latrine closet - the one you saw outside projecting from the round tower. This reasonably appointed chamber was probably the **Duke's Chamber**, where he actually slept (his great bed down in his hall was used more for entertaining).

The Duke's Chamber, where Albany would normally have slept.

Continuing up the spiral stair you reach a curved passage. Along that passage a door on the right leads into a room almost identical to the Duke's Chamber below, except that it is not *en suite*. This was probably the **Duchess's Chamber**, where she slept. Her latrine was somewhat clumsily located outside the chamber next to the spiral stair.

The Duchess's Hall

Just beyond the Duchess's Chamber is the spacious room known as the **Duchess's Hall**. It has the same dimensions as her husband's below, and would have been similarly decorated and furnished. Heating was provided by a fireplace in the east wall; although fragmentary, it seems to have had moulded jambs similar to those on the fireplace in the Duke's Hall, only turned outwards to support a projecting hood. Midway along the courtyard wall is an alcove that would once have been screened off from the hall. This was the **oratory**, or private chapel, for in the east wall there is a triangular-headed credence, for holding the consecrated vessels, and an octagonal *piscina* for washing them; both would have been to the right of the small altar. In the opposite wall, a small opening has been made to enable the Duchess's ladies-in-waiting in the adjacent window recess to watch the service. The large window in the south-east corner of the hall has a doorway leading to the wall-walk.

The credence and basin in the Duchess's oratory on the second floor.

Projecting stone corbels in the side walls of the Duchess's Hall indicate where the ceiling once was. The topmost floor seems to have been divided into smaller chambers and closets, probably for use by members of Albanys' family as well as their chiefs of staff. A man such as Albany would have had a permanent household well in excess of 50 souls, all requiring somewhere to sleep. Whilst the most menial servants bedded down in the great hall and kitchen, others further up the social ladder were given beds in the many nooks and crannies throughout the castle.

Return to the spiral stair and continue up to the **battlements** of the gatehouse tower. Standing here you can appreciate the magnificent setting Albany chose for his new home. The views out over his vast earldom were an important part of the concept of lordship in medieval times - 'see and be seen'. Certainly, whether you are admiring the views from the castle, or the walls of the castle from the outside, you are left in no doubt of the importance of the mighty duke who built Doune Castle.

The Story of Doune Castle

Doune Castle was built towards the end of the fourteenth century by a man who would be king, Robert Stewart, Duke of Albany. Albany was at the centre of the maelstrom of Scottish political life for 50 years, ruling in the place of a weak brother and an incapacitated nephew. But it is for his role in the death of one heir to the throne and the imprisonment of another that he is best remembered, perhaps unfairly.

Albany, a scion of the royal house of Stewart, held the reins of government of Scotland for almost 20 years until his death in 1420 at the ripe old age of 80. He was known by his contemporaries as 'a big spender'. His mighty castle at Doune, beside the River Teith, is tangible proof of that.

Albany never saw his dream for Doune fully realised. It was left to future Stewart sovereigns to enjoy the unfinished fortress-residence begun by the man known to history as 'Scotland's uncrowned king'.

Doune Castle from the south east with the snow-capped peak of Beinn Deorg and the Menteith Hills beyond. The seal is that of Robert, Duke of Albany and Earl of Fife and Menteith (S(igillum) roberti:ducis:albanie:comitis:de:ffye:et:de:menteth)

A Dun Called 'Doune'

Doune Castle from the east looking up the River Teith towards the Menteith Hills. The peak of Ben Lomond can be seen on the horizon (top left).

Doune Castle is strategically sited on a promontory formed by the meeting of the River Teith and the Ardoch Burn. The importance of the location was clearly recognised from very early times, judging by the evidence of prehistoric activity in the area. The Romans certainly appreciated the strength of the position for in the first century AD, shortly after Governor Agricola's invasion, his legionaries constructed a fort of timber and earth on the level ground just to the north of the castle, between the castle and the present village of Doune. The level ground that attracted the Roman army has since proved equally attractive to Doune Cricket Club!

Whether there was a fortification on the site of the present Doune Castle in prehistoric or Dark-Age times can only be solved through excavation. But the name 'Doune' suggests that this was the case. The word derives from 'dun', meaning an ancient stronghold, and the ditches and banks that cross the promontory may well belong to an earlier fort. That there was a castle on the site before Albany's time in the late fourteenth century is suggested by the clues in the lower part of the kitchen tower (see page 7).

Doune commands a bend in the fast-flowing waters of the River Teith.

Albany - 'Big Spender'

"Quiet authority accomplishes what violence cannot."
(Abbot Walter Bower of Inchcolm, in his obituary of Robert Stewart, Duke of Albany, published around 1440)

"[Albany] was the most patient of men, gentle enough and kind, talkative and friendly, a daily attender at feasts, outstanding beside all his companions, a man who was a big spender and generous to strangers. He was also distinguished in appearance, tall and lofty in body, grey-haired and understanding, loving in countenance, gifted with prudence and bravery, famous for his discretion, unremitting in his forebearance. And so in him wisdom provided the ornament of nearly all the virtues, so that his discourse whether delivered in the highest councils of the kingdom or elsewhere was always seasoned with charm and wit."

History has been unkind to Robert Stewart, Duke of Albany. He is remembered as the man who was all but king for almost 50 chaotic years until his death in 1420, and who, many have argued, held on to that position only by murdering one nephew, David Duke of Rothesay, and failing to aid the release from captivity of another, James I. But history is always written by the winning side, and in the end James I won.

In order to understand the man, we must first sketch in a little of the historical background. His father, Robert II, the first of the Stewart dynasty, came to the throne in 1371 aged 55. He was gentle but ineffectual. The one thing he was good at, it would appear, was fathering children - he had at least 21, though only four were legitimate at birth. Robert II had lived with Elizabeth Mure of Rowallan for a decade before the belated papal dispensation for the marriage and legitimisation of their children arrived in 1347. It was the children of this first liaison, including our Robert Stewart, who inherited his power and dominated Scotland for a generation and more.

Finding sufficient lands and titles for this considerable family began the 'Stewartisation' of the Highlands, a process that was to prove both costly and divisive throughout the reign of his eldest son, Robert III, Robert Stewart's big brother. The chronicler, Walter Bower, wrote kindly of Robert II, 'but what', he added 'shall I say of his sons? Some were peaceable and benign, some insolent and malign'. The failure of both King Roberts to control law and order and spending amongst their kinsmen led to the nobility of Scotland placing a greater reliance on the shoulders of Robert II's infinitely more capable second son, Robert Stewart.

Robert Stewart was born before 1340. His marriage in 1361 to Margaret Graham, heiress of the Menteith estates, brought him that earldom, with its island stronghold of Inch Talla on the Lake of Menteith. A decade later he acquired the earldom of Fife, with its magnificent castle at Falkland. By the time he was appointed chamberlain in 1382, he was already established as a strong politician.

Four years later 'the great and many defects in the governance of the realm' - the result of the weakness of his father and the infirmity of his elder brother - led to Robert Stewart's elevation to the governorship of Scotland, an appointment he was to hold for the remainder of his life, except for the three years between 1399 and 1402 when his nephew, the Duke of Rothesay, challenged his authority. But Robert's appointment was hedged with mistrust.

Initially, Robert was appointed for a year and charged to behave 'well and usefully in the aforesaid office'. Throughout his time as governor, the politics of greed, envy, intrigue and fear dominated. But putting matters into a European context, this was an age when even popes disagreed with each other - all three of them at one point! Also, the political map of Scotland was very different then. The Northern Isles remained under Norwegian sovereignty, in the west the MacDonald Lord of the Isles still harboured treasonable ambitions (even though he was a cousin of the king), whilst southern Scotland was dominated by families who had long mastered the art of getting their way by real or threatened negotiations with successive English kings. And England still had designs on Scotland. Against this backdrop, it is perhaps surprising that Robert Stewart managed to survive to the ripe old age of 80.

The record of Robert Stewart's governorship certainly leaves mixed messages about the man. That he strengthened his family's position, both politically and financially, is not in doubt. But that should be seen against the politics of the day. Certainly his contemporaries did not judge him harshly, with Bower, in his obituary, describing him as 'the most patient of all men, gentle enough and kind, talkative and friendly, a daily attender at feasts, outstanding beside all his companions, generous to strangers, loveable in countenance, gifted with prudence and bravery, famous for his discretion, unremitting in his forbearance'.
In his time as governor, he did so much that was good, including presiding over the founding of Scotland's first university at St Andrews. How come, then, he has had such a bad press ever since?

The longest shadow over Robert Stewart's governorship will remain the death in 1402 of his nephew and the heir to the throne, David Duke of Rothesay, whilst in Robert's care at Falkland - 'some say of dysentery and some of starvation.' Conflict between the two was well-known and had led to them both receiving the first Scottish dukedoms ever awarded, in a vain attempt by their father the king to keep the peace between them. Yet even in the title Robert chose, he betrayed his ambitions, for Albany, or Alba, had been the name of the ancient kingdom of Scotland. Albany was not actually present at his nephew's death, and the king declared that he was innocent of any involvement and that there should be no 'muttering' against him; but the muttering continues to this day.

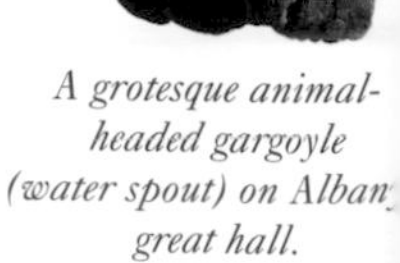

A grotesque animal-headed gargoyle (water spout) on Albany's great hall.

From the time in 1406 when the English captured another of Albany's nephews, James, the heir to the throne, to the time in 1420 when he passed away, Albany was effectively both heir presumptive and regent of Scotland. That he had ambitions to become

king himself one day was betrayed in an indenture he sealed in 1409 for it contained the phrase 'gif it happynnis the said lorde, Duc Albany, to grow in tyme to the estate of king'. Whilst there is no direct evidence that Albany dragged his feet over the negotiations to free James I from captivity, James clearly felt Albany's heart was not in it.

Albany's ambition, probably long-held, must have influenced the building of Doune Castle, for the accommodation provided is very similar to that found in any major royal castle of the time. Certainly money was no object; as Bower noted in his obituary, Albany was 'a big spender'. The planning of Doune continued the tradition of the great thirteenth-century enclosure castles such as Bothwell and Caerlaverock, but foreshadowed the impressive courtyard palaces of Linlithgow and Falkland that followed. Certainly Doune displays the proper regard for defence that would be expected, whilst providing well-planned and hierarchical accommodation. The first references to Doune Castle occur in documents dated 1381, and it was presumably habitable by 1401 when Albany wrote letters from there to Henry IV of England.

A 'Maist Pleasant' Royal House

Albany died without realising his royal ambition; he has passed into the pages of history with the soubriquet 'Scotland's uncrowned king'. He left a poor inheritance, for his own son and heir, Murdoch, displayed none of his father's strengths whilst excelling in his frailties. On his father's death Murdoch inherited the governorship, but, given the deep mistrust James I had for Albany, there was inevitably going to be a 'show-down' on James's return. That came in 1424, and within the year Murdoch's head had parted company with his shoulders. Murdoch's own son and his father-in-law were executed at the same time. James I was determined that 'the key should keep the castle and the bracken bush the cow, though I myself lead the life of a dog in bringing it to pass'. Scotland, and with it Doune Castle, reverted to the Crown.

Royal keepers were now appointed to maintain the castle in readiness for their king's coming. Each had at his disposal income derived from certain lands, fishings and mills on the estate, to pay for staff and provisions, and also for repairs. The payments were now dutifully recorded in the royal accounts. Alas, the picture they paint is hardly one that Albany envisaged for his castle. It seems that Doune Castle was seen as a useful retreat, to be kept in repair, but not used often enough to warrant significant expenditure. Between 1430 and 1581 we find only the following repairs carried out - to the stables in 1434, and the doors and beds in 1467; a brewery was built in the same year.
It is not until the late sixteenth century that any major works were undertaken and they were clearly as a result of long neglect.

Doune's proximity to Stirling Castle, and to the hunting forests of Glenfinlas, near Callander, and in the Braes of Menteith, near Aberfoyle, made it an attractive hunting-lodge.

The castle's pleasing location probably also ensured its frequent inclusion in the marriage portion of successive queens. James II's queen, Mary of Gueldres, was granted it in 1449, James III's queen, Margaret of Denmark, in 1468 (in part-exchange for the remaining Norwegian lands in the Northern Isles that she brought to the marriage), and James IV's queen, Margaret Tudor, in 1503. Each in turn seems to have spent at least some time in residence at Doune during her widowhood.

Their stay would have been pleasant. Records tell of beasts and poultry being delivered for the royal table. In 1448, a princely sum was spent on seeds for the castle gardens, and a decade later John Hemrici, the gardener, was paid to plant onions, cabbages and leeks.

Other members of the household included a chaplain (serving the two chapels of St Fillan, one inside the castle and the other beyond the present village of Doune), a tailor, laundress, porter and watchmen, and a 'keeper of the meadows'.

It was James VI who gave a new lease of life to Doune. In 1581, aged 15, he opined that 'at our last repairing [retiring] towart our castell and place of Doune in Menteith, we persavit [perceived] the samin and fields thereabout to be maist pleasant for our pastyme and verray commodious for our dwelling in the symmer season'. But he went on to outline the perilous state of the walls and roofs and commanded its keeper to spend the then considerable sum of £200 on the repair; in the event, the works cost considerably more. The craftsmanship of Michael Ewing, the stonemason, is here to be enjoyed yet, in the corbelled-out parapet atop the curtain walls and those attractive round turrets. The slates put on the main roofs by someone called Makquarren have long since been replaced.

Mighty Doune Castle, seen here from the north east, was first visited by James VI (pictured above in a painting by Adrian Vanson) in 1580. On leaving, he gave orders that the royal castle be refurbished as a base from where he could pursue those country 'pastimes', chiefly hunting, that he much loved indulging in throughout his long life.

Royal Keepers

William Moray is the first recorded royal keeper of Doune. In 1434, Moray was made responsible for providing for the upkeep and protection of the castle, using income derived from lands, fishings and mills on the estate. The Morays continued as keepers until 1468, when the post passed to Edmonstoun of Drumcampsy, who was permitted to appoint constables, jailers, guards and other officials. Charters to the successive keepers were issued almost annually into the seventeenth century. But an ill-judged act by William Edmonstoun of Duntreath saw the keepership pass to the Stewarts. It has remained with them ever since.

In 1525, James IV's widowed Queen Margaret wrote to Sir William Edmonstoun instructing him to prepare the castle for her arrival. He replied that he would do so, but that there was room only for her majesty and her gentlewomen; the rest of her retinue would have to stay elsewhere. The queen took this as a refusal to fulfil his duties, and upon her remarriage two years later to Henry Stewart, Lord Methven, she removed Edmonstoun from office and installed her new brother-in-law, Sir James Stewart of Beath, as keeper. Sir James proved incapable of making the most of his new-found wealth and status, and he died in a street brawl in Dunblane in 1544.

Sir James's son, also James, who succeeded him as keeper, fared little better. Implicated in the murder of David Riccio, Mary Queen of Scots' favourite, in Holyrood Palace in 1565, he was later accused of supporting her following her abdication in 1567. He was ordered to forfeit Doune. He refused, and an army under Regent Lennox's command laid siege to the castle - the first in its 200-year history. After three days Stewart surrendered the castle on condition that it would not be destroyed. Once in Lennox's hands, the castle was used to imprison and torture a servant, John Moon, accused of having 'dangerous dealings' with England. During the civil war in the 1570s, the castle saw regular service as a prison, holding several troublesome Border figures, including Sir Walter Scott of Branxholm. They were joined by the commendator of Paisley Abbey and several Edinburgh bailies.

In time Sir James Stewart was reinstated as keeper and created Lord Doune in 1570; his rehabilitation was complete when he married Elizabeth Stewart, daughter and heir of the Earl of Moray. His heirs became the earls of Moray, and Doune Castle has remained theirs ever since.

Doune was last used during the 1745 Jacobite Rising, when it was held for Prince Charles Edward Stewart by McGregor of Glengyle and a garrison of 25 men. After the Jacobite victory at Falkirk early in 1746, McGregor's men took delivery of 150 redcoats. Some were imprisoned in the tower above the kitchen, and six escaped by knotting bed-sheets together and lowering themselves from the window; the last to escape had to jump when the makeshift rope broke. One of the escapees, John Home, later wrote of the escapade in his *History of the Rebellion*. Home also went on to become a leading London dramatist; his Covent Garden premier of *Douglas* was received with rapturous applause, during which one carried-away member of the audience was heard to exclaim "Whaur's yer Wully Shakespeare noo?".

The castle fell out of use after this, and by the end of the century it was ruinous. It remained so until 1883 when the fourteenth Earl of Moray appointed an architect, Andrew Kerr, to carry out an inspection of the castle and restore it. The Great Hall and Duke's Hall are the most obvious signs of their handiwork. In 1970, the Moray estate leased the castle to the state, and Doune is now cared for by Historic Scotland.

Doune Castle, as illustrated by Robert Billings around 1850, before the major restoration carried out by the 14th Earl of Moray. Note the absence of a well-head in the courtyard and roofs anywhere.

FURTHER READING

W D Simpson *Doune Castle, Proceedings of the Society of Antiquaries of Scotland* (1938)

R Fawcett *Scottish Architecture from the Accession of the Stewarts to the Reformation, 1371-1560* (1994)

C Tabraham *Scotland's Castles* (1997)

D E R Watt (ed) *A History Book for Scots* (1998)

J G Dunbar *Scottish Royal Palaces* (1999)

J Gifford and F A Walker *Buildings of Scotland - Stirling and Central Scotland* (2002)